My Horse Riding Journal

By Olivia Grace

Copyright

derived from various sources. Please consult a licensed professional before attempting any techniques outlined in this book.

By reading this document, the reader agrees that under no circumstances is the author responsible for any losses, direct or indirect, which are incurred because of the use of information contained within this document, including, but not limited to, —errors, omissions, or inaccuracies.

Introduction

Hi Girls

Welcome to your new Horse-Riding Journal!

My daughter Gracie is mad about horses and she is now a very keen rider. With all the different experiences that she has had during her lessons she needed somewhere to write it all down, and so we made her this journal. We thought you would like one too.

Within this awesome book you will be able to:

- Record what you have learnt and what date you learnt it, so that you can look back and remember

- Draw or stick in photos of you and your favourite horse to ride
- Color: some of our favourite horse pictures
- Read some great horse poetry
- And record all your thoughts and feelings on what is a truly amazing hobby.

Are you ready to start recording?

"Under Starters orders...ready...GO!

Draw Your Favourite Horse!

Stick in a picture of your horse

HERE!

Riding Day

Date:_____

Name:_____

Height:_____HH

Age:_____

Color:_____

Notes_____

_____

_____

_____

_____

_____

_____

_____

_____

_____

_____

_____

_____

_____

_____

_____

_____

_____

_____

_____

_____

_____

_____

_____

_____

_____

_____

Things to Remember

_____

_____

_____

_____

_____

_____

_____

Riding Day

Date:_____

Name:_____

Height:_____HH

Age:_____

Color:_____

Notes_____

_____

_____

_____

_____

_____

_____

_____

_____

_____

_____

_____

_____

_____

_____

_____

_____

_____

_____

_____

_____

_____

_____

_____

_____

_____

_____

Things to Remember

_____

_____

_____

_____

_____

_____

_____

Riding Day

Date:_____

Name:_____

Height:_____HH

Age:_____

Color:_____

Notes_____
_____
_____
_____
_____
_____
_____
_____
_____

_____

_____

_____

_____

_____

_____

_____

_____

_____

_____

_____

_____

_____

_____

_____

_____

_____

_____

Things to Remember

_____

_____

_____

_____

_____

_____

_____

_____

Riding Day

Date:_____

Name:_____

Height:_____HH

Age:_____

Color:_____

Notes_____

_____

_____

_____

_____

_____

_____

_____

_____

_____

_____

_____

_____

_____

_____

_____

_____

_____

_____

_____

_____

_____

_____

_____

_____

_____

_____

_____

Things to Remember

_____

_____

_____

_____

_____

_____

_____

Riding Day

Date:_____

Name:_____

Height:_____HH

Age:_____

Color:_____

Notes_____

_____

_____

_____

_____

_____

_____

_____

_____

_____

_____

_____

_____

_____

_____

_____

_____

_____

_____

_____

_____

_____

_____

_____

_____

_____

Things to Remember

_____

_____

_____

_____

_____

_____

_____

Horse Quiz for 'Horse Mad' Riders

This quiz helps you to work out whether or not you are really, really Horse Mad. There are some people that just like horses. There are some people that just put up with horses. There are some people that just pretend to like horses because everyone else does. We need to make sure that you are really HORSE MAD! To help us do this please answer the questions below.

Go through it with a friend if you need to!

1.   What do you dream of when you go to sleep?
     a) Cuddly Toys
     b) Chocolate
     c) Horses

2.   What do you really want for Christmas?
     a) iPad
     b) Hover Board
     c) Horse

3.   What is your bedroom wall covered with?
     a) Your favourite Pop Star
     b) Pictures of Horses
     c) Nothing

4. What programs do you always look for when you go on Netflix?
   a) Cartoons
   b) Horse Films
   c) Disney

5. What programs do you always look for when you go on YouTube?
   a) How to draw Horses
   b) Computer games
   c) Music Videos

6. When you are in the car staring out the window, what would cause you to scream out and make everyone aware if you saw one?
   a) A horse
   b) A dog
   c) A cat

7. When you have time to draw whatever you want, what
    do you draw?

    a) Cartoon Pictures

    b) Horses

    c) Princesses

8. What animal was in the last two books you read?

    a) Horse

    b) Dog

    c) Frog

9. You sleep with a fluffy toy which is a...?

    a) Bear

    b) Horse/Unicorn

    c) Dinosaur

10. What animal is on your favourite T-shirt?

   a) Deer

   b) Horse/Unicorn

   c) Dog

If most of your answers are the word Horse or Unicorn then I have the honour of telling you that quite positively, quite absolutely, you are HORSE MAD!

Why be part of the "Horse Mad Girls Club"?

Stick in a Photograph of You Horse Riding!

My Notes

Riding Day

Date:_____

Name:_____

Height:_____HH

Age:_____

Color:_____

Notes_____
_____
_____
_____
_____
_____
_____
_____
_____
_____

Things to Remember

Riding Day

Date:_____

Name:_____

Height:_____HH

Age:_____

Color:_____

Notes_____

_____

_____

_____

_____

_____

_____

_____

_____

_____

_____

_____

_____

_____

_____

_____

_____

_____

_____

_____

_____

_____

_____

_____

_____

_____

_____

Things to Remember

_____

_____

_____

_____

_____

_____

_____

_____

Riding Day

Date:_____

Name:_____

Height:_____HH

Age:_____

Color:_____

Notes_____

_____

_____

_____

_____

_____

_____

_____

_____

_____

Things to Remember

Riding Day

Date:_____

Name:_____

Height:_____HH

Age:_____

Color:_____

Notes_____
_____
_____
_____
_____
_____
_____
_____
_____

_____

_____

_____

_____

_____

_____

_____

_____

_____

_____

_____

_____

_____

_____

_____

_____

_____

Things to Remember

_____

_____

_____

_____

_____

_____

_____

_____

Riding Day

Date:_____

Name:_____

Height:_____HH

Age:_____

Color:_____

Notes_____

_____

_____

_____

_____

_____

_____

_____

_____

_____

Things to Remember

Poem Corner

Horses

By Steve Hanson

My horse is really smart.
There's so much he can do.
He knows how to chop carrots
and cook them in a stew.

My horse can make my bed
and dust shelves with his tail.
And when he paints the hall,
he masters each detail.

I want to keep him inside—
there's so much to be gained
except for one small detail:
he isn't potty trained!

Fly Away Horse

By Eugene Field

Oh, a wonderful horse is the Fly-Away Horse--
Perhaps you have seen him before;
Perhaps, while you slept, his shadow has swept
Through the moonlight that floats on the floor.
For it's only at night, when the stars twinkle bright,
That the Fly-Away Horse, with a neigh
And a pull at his rein and a toss of his mane,
Is up on his heels and away!
The moon in the sky,
As he gallopeth by,
Cries: "Oh! What a marvelous sight!"
And the Stars in dismay
Hide their faces away
In the lap of old Grandmother Night.

It is yonder, out yonder, the Fly-Away Horse
Speedeth ever and ever away--
Over meadows and lane, over mountains and plains,
Over streamlets that sing at their play;
And over the sea like a ghost sweepeth he,
While the ships they go sailing below,

And he speedeth so fast that the men on the mast

Adjudge him some portent of woe.

"What ho, there!" they cry,

As he flourishes by

With a whisk of his beautiful tail;

And the fish in the sea

Are as scared as can be,

From the nautilus up to the whale!

And the Fly-Away Horse seeks those far-away lands

You little folk dream of at night--

Where candy-trees grow, and honey-brooks flow,

And corn-fields with popcorn are white;

And the beasts in the wood are ever so good

To children who visit them there--

What glory astride of a lion to ride,

Or to wrestle around with a bear!

The monkeys, they say:

"Come on, let us play,"

And they frisk in the coconut-trees:

While the parrots, that cling

To the peanut-vines sing

Or converse with comparative ease!

Off! scamper to bed -- you shall ride him to-night!

For, as soon as you've fallen asleep,

With a jubilant neigh he shall bear you away

Over forest and hillside and deep!

But tell us, my dear, all you see and you hear

In those beautiful lands over there,

Where the Fly-Away Horse wings his far-away course

With the wee one consigned to his care.

Then grandma will cry

In amazement: "Oh, my!"

And she'll think it could never be so.

And only we two

Shall know it is true--

You and I, little precious! shall know!

Riding Day

Date:_____

Name:_____

Height:_____HH

Age:_____

Color:_____

Notes_____
_____
_____
_____
_____
_____
_____
_____
_____
_____

_____

_____

_____

_____

_____

_____

_____

_____

_____

_____

_____

_____

_____

_____

_____

_____

Things to Remember

_____

_____

_____

_____

_____

_____

_____

_____

Riding Day

Date:_____

Name:_____

Height:_____HH

Age:_____

Color:_____

Notes_____

_____

_____

_____

_____

_____

_____

_____

_____

_____

_____

_____

_____

_____

_____

_____

_____

_____

_____

_____

_____

_____

_____

_____

_____

_____

_____

_____

_____

Things to Remember

_____

_____

_____

_____

_____

_____

_____

_____

Riding Day

Date:_____

Name:_____

Height:_____HH

Age:_____

Color:_____

Notes_____

_____

_____

_____

_____

_____

_____

_____

_____

_____

_____

_____

_____

_____

_____

_____

_____

_____

_____

_____

_____

_____

_____

_____

_____

_____

Things to Remember

_____

_____

_____

_____

_____

_____

_____

_____

Riding Day

Date:_____

Name:_____

Height:_____HH

Age:_____

Color:_____

Notes_____

_____

_____

_____

_____

_____

_____

_____

_____

_____

_____

_____

_____

_____

_____

_____

_____

_____

_____

_____

_____

_____

_____

_____

_____

_____

_____

_____

Things to Remember

_____

_____

_____

_____

_____

_____

_____

_____

Riding Day

Date:_____

Name:_____

Height:_____HH

Age:_____

Color:_____

Notes_____

_____

_____

_____

_____

_____

_____

_____

_____

_____

_____

_____

_____

_____

_____

_____

_____

_____

_____

_____

_____

_____

_____

_____

_____

_____

_____

Things to Remember

_____

_____

_____

_____

_____

_____

_____

_____

_____

Fun Horse Facts

- Horses can sleep both lying down and standing up

- Horses can lift up to around 25 human years long

- A 19ᵗʰ Century Horse named "Old Billy" is said to have lived 62 years

- Horses have around 205 bones in their body

- Horses only eat plants, making them herbivores

- A male horse is called a stallion and a female horse is called a mare

- A group of horses will not go to sleep at the same time, at least one will stay awake to look after the others

- Like humans' horses have different facial expressions to express how they are feeling

- Sampson the Shire horse was the tallest horse on record. He was 21.2 hands high!

Coloring Pages

Coloring Pages

Coloring Pages

Coloring Pages

Riding Day

Date:_____

Name:_____

Height:_____HH

Age:_____

Color:_____

Notes_____

_____

_____

_____

_____

_____

_____

_____

_____

_____

_____

_____

_____

_____

_____

_____

_____

_____

_____

_____

_____

_____

_____

_____

_____

_____

_____

_____

Things to Remember

_____

_____

_____

_____

_____

_____

_____

_____

Riding Day

Date:_____

Name:_____

Height:_____HH

Age:_____

Color:_____

Notes_____

_____

_____

_____

_____

_____

_____

_____

_____

_____

_____

_____

_____

_____

_____

_____

_____

_____

_____

_____

_____

_____

_____

_____

_____

Things to Remember

_____

_____

_____

_____

_____

_____

_____

Riding Day

Date:_____

Name:_____

Height:_____HH

Age:_____

Color:_____

Notes_____
_____
_____
_____
_____
_____
_____
_____
_____
_____

_____

_____

_____

_____

_____

_____

_____

_____

_____

_____

_____

_____

_____

_____

_____

_____

_____

Things to Remember

_____

_____

_____

_____

_____

_____

_____

_____

Riding Day

Date:_____

Name:_____

Height:_____HH

Age:_____

Color:_____

Notes_____

_____

_____

_____

_____

_____

_____

_____

_____

_____

_____

_____

_____

_____

_____

_____

_____

_____

_____

_____

_____

_____

_____

_____

_____

Things to Remember

_____

_____

_____

_____

_____

_____

_____

_____

Riding Day

Date:_____

Name:_____

Height:_____HH

Age:_____

Color:_____

Notes_____

_____

_____

_____

_____

_____

_____

_____

_____

Things to Remember

Riding Day

Date:_____

Name:_____

Height:_____HH

Age:_____

Color:_____

Notes_____
_____
_____
_____
_____
_____
_____
_____
_____

_____
_____
_____
_____
_____
_____
_____
_____
_____
_____
_____
_____
_____
_____
_____
_____
_____

Things to Remember

_____
_____
_____
_____
_____
_____
_____

Riding Day

Date:_____

Name:_____

Height:_____HH

Age:_____

Color:_____

Notes_____

_____

_____

_____

_____

_____

_____

_____

_____

Things to Remember

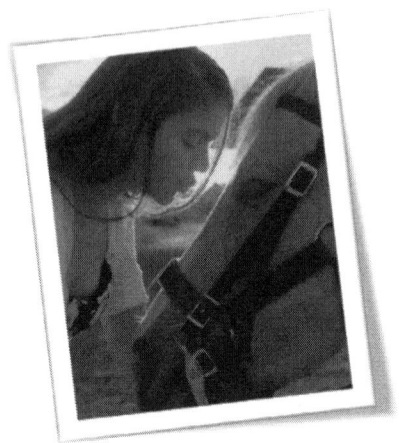

Riding Day

Date:_____

Name:_____

Height:_____HH

Age:_____

Color:_____

Notes_____

_____

_____

_____

_____

_____

_____

_____

_____

_____

Things to Remember

Riding Day

Date:_____

Name:_____

Height:_____HH

Age:_____

Color:_____

Notes_____
_____
_____
_____
_____
_____
_____
_____
_____

Things to Remember

Riding Day

Date:_____

Name:_____

Height:_____HH

Age:_____

Color:_____

Notes_____
_____
_____
_____
_____
_____
_____
_____
_____

Things to Remember

Riding Day

Date:_____

Name:_____

Height:_____HH

Age:_____

Color:_____

Notes_____

_____

_____

_____

_____

_____

_____

_____

_____

Things to Remember

Riding Day

Date:_____

Name:_____

Height:_____HH

Age:_____

Color:_____

Notes_____
_____
_____
_____
_____
_____
_____
_____
_____

_____

_____

_____

_____

_____

_____

_____

_____

_____

_____

_____

_____

_____

_____

_____

_____

_____

Things to Remember

_____

_____

_____

_____

_____

_____

_____

_____

Riding Day

Date:_____

Name:_____

Height:_____HH

Age:_____

Color:_____

Notes_____

_____

_____

_____

_____

_____

_____

_____

_____

_____

_____

_____

_____

_____

_____

_____

_____

_____

_____

_____

_____

_____

_____

Things to Remember

_____

_____

_____

_____

_____

_____

_____

Riding Day

Date:_____

Name:_____

Height:_____HH

Age:_____

Color:_____

Notes_____

_____

_____

_____

_____

_____

_____

_____

_____

_____

_____

_____

_____

_____

_____

_____

_____

_____

_____

_____

_____

_____

_____

_____

_____

Things to Remember

_____

_____

_____

_____

_____

_____

_____

_____

Riding Day

Date:_____

Name:_____

Height:_____HH

Age:_____

Color:_____

Notes_____
_____
_____
_____
_____
_____
_____
_____

_____

_____

_____

_____

_____

_____

_____

_____

_____

_____

_____

_____

_____

_____

_____

_____

_____

_____

Things to Remember

_____

_____

_____

_____

_____

_____

_____

_____

Important Horse Terms to Know!

Ancestor

A member of the family that lived a long time ago

Bit

The part of the bridle that goes into the horse's mouth

Blacksmith

A Blacksmith is someone who makes things with iron. Sometimes this can be horse shoes.

Breeding Stock

A mare or stallion that is intended for breeding work. They are normally chosen because of their good qualities.

Bridle

A piece of horse headgear made up of leather straps

Curry Comb

A square or rectangular or oval comb with rubber or

plastic teeth used for
grooming horses

Dam   A Mother Horse

Dandy Brush   A brush with harsh wiry
                        bristles used for grooming
                        horses.

Domesticated   An animal that is used to
                        living alongside humans

Farrier   A farrier is a blacksmith that
                        does horseshoeing but
                        doesn't necessarily do other
                        work with iron.

Gelding   A male horse that has had an
                        operation to stop it
                        producing offspring

Hogging   A Horse mane that has been
                        completely shaved

Holter   Horse headgear that is

	sometimes made of rope.
Listless	Lifeless; not wanting to do anything
Mare	An Adult female horse
Muzzle	The sticking out part of an animal's face that includes their nose and mouth.
Stallion	An Adult horse that can produce offspring
RoughAge:	Fibre from grasses and other long-stemmed plants
Steeplechase	A horse race over an obstacle course or open country
Taut	Stretched or Tightened
Turnout	The time when the horse is out of the confinement of the

stable and loose in a larger
area.

Withers   The top of a horse's shoulder
blade

Additional Journal Notes

Drawing PAge:s

Drawing PAge:s

Drawing PAge:s

Drawing Pages

Drawing PAge:s

Printed in Great
Britain
by Amazon